Michael R. Clark

The Highly Acclaimed Author of "The Struggle Stops Here."

PRESENTS

CONDITION YOURSELF FOR SUCCESS

"OVER 110 SUGGESTIONS FOR A MORE FULFILLING AND POWERFUL LIFE".

CLARK ASSOCIATED BUSINESSES

To my son Taylor Reuben Clark this book is dedicated. At the ripe young age of four years he showed the wisdom, compassion and thoughtfulness one would expect from someone ten times his age. With each passing day he shows the world more of the same. God has truly blessed Taylor and he is destined to do great things.

Acknowledgements

• • • • •

There are so many people who have made this writing and my work possible! An acknowledgement of their support would be the very least I should convey. First, I must thank the 600 plus young people involved in the S.T.A.R. Program of Baltimore City. In their own unique way, each one of them has inspired me and my staff.

This writing actually could not have been possible without the input of Brenda Williams who helped me to view motivational concepts from many different perspectives. Her insight leaves an indelible impression upon my work. Mr. Marvin Mack, founder of the Center for Mind and Esteem Development, Inc., has conferred with me on many occasions. Each time we converse, I am enriched.

Chris Heidelberg and Tony Reid are two of the most talented personal development experts I know. They exhibit an indepth knowledge of their craft and know how to captivate their audiences with every word. From both, I have learned much. Craig Thompson, a brilliant young motivational speaker is redefining what motivational concepts are all about and I thank him for inspiring me on many occasions.

Gail Cuffie is the one all must learn from. She has taught me the importance of faith, sincerity and Godliness. Gail is tomorrow's personal development superstar. Phil Stewart is like a missionary when it comes to personal empowerment. He enthusiastically spreads the word to those who are just starting to understand the power of personal development. No one expresses the importance of personal empowerment like Phil.

I would be remiss if I did not thank Donata Griffin for her tireless effort on the manuscript for this work, and Lavinia Jackson for fine tuning much of the work. I also must acknowledge the following people for their continued support and dedication to the art of personal empowerment: Harold Adams–El, Myrna Adejoh, Gregory Cameron, Henry Daniyan, Cheryl Harris, Pauline Jenkins, Peter Mensah, Ryan Moore, Kim Rivers, Carmilla Stokes, Akua Zenzele, Linda Ellard, Amber Nash, Graeme Gates, Christopher Wafer and Corey Anderson.

Introduction

• • • • •

In my first book, THE STRUGGLE STOPS HERE, I introduced ten fundamental keys to attaining greater levels of success in life. I outlined those "keys to success" and discussed each one individually. In this book, I decided to go beyond the fundamentals and present a cadre of personal empowerment information designed to enlighten and inspire the reader. You will find many inspiring stories as well as indepth concepts which illustrate specific personal development principles.

I was blessed with the opportunity to share many of my self-empowerment concepts with tens of thousands of television viewers in the Baltimore/Washington area each morning, as my audience prepared for their day. Through the visual media, I dispensed a message of hope and personal empowerment to help individuals meet the challenges of the day. In this book, you will find many of the inspiring stories I shared in my more than one hundred television appearances. Countless letters, requesting the material presented on the air, have been forwarded to me. I spent nearly a year putting my words to print. At times it was an arduous process converting the verbal stories to print, while trying to retain the impact of the tale being told. However, with the help of some special friends and associates I believe the task was done well.

My recommendation to anyone who chooses to read this book is to read it slowly and sagaciously. Let the inspiring concepts sink into your soul. Re–read the stories several times. Let them become a part of you and you become a part of them. The concepts will guide you to a greater, more positive and fulfilling life, for these concepts are actually "seeds of life."

Each of us is a farmer in our own right. We plant seeds into the "soil" of our soul from the moment we take our first breath. Initially, the seeds we plant are often handed to us by someone else, perhaps a friend or a loved one. However, at a very early age we learn the art of cultivation and begin to select our own seeds. This book is full of great seeds, seeds that you can add to your spreader as you prepare your field of life.

"SUCCESS IS NOT HAPHAZARD!
IT IS ACHIEVED THROUGH A
CONDITIONING PROCESS!"

— M. Clark

The Level of Your Success
· · · · ·

Many factors in life, such as hard work, diligence and your determination will influence the level of your success. All of these factors are very important, but the most important factor, by far, is your attitude, and the way in which you believe in your own ability.

If we find excuses for why something will not work for us, then we have found the perfect way to stop something from working for us. Excuses are never difficult to ascertain when we need one to justify why something will not or cannot work.

However, if we are dedicated to finding a solution, we will find one every time. The first step, of course, is believing that you can find the solution and starting your search based on that belief.

When You Believe in You

• • • • •

There are many people who will believe in you and your abilities, however, the most important believer must be you. Your family and friends may say how much they support and believe in your talents and abilities. This is absolutely necessary support, but, it is you who must convince yourself that you truly believe in your own ability.

There is nothing, and no one (except you) to keep you from believing, 100 percent, that you can accomplish whatever your goals in life may be. You have to be a strong self–supporter because no one will have more influence on the outcome of your life than you.

When you believe in you, the negatives that often present themselves as roadblocks, begin to appear as mere pebbles and you will feel as though you're driving a steam roller over them. Negative roadblocks will be no match for you – when you believe in you.

Learn to Recognize the Riches You Possess

• • • • •

There was once a struggling Herdsmen who lived in Egypt. He wanted to find the great wealth. So, he sold everything he owned, including all of his cattle, sheep and land. (He heard stories of great fortunes in gold being found all over his country.) Then he, with a back pack full of supplies, went out to find a fortune in gold.

A few years later he found himself penniless, hopeless and distraught, so he jumped off a bridge and drowned himself. One day the Herdsman who acquired his land found an abandoned cave as he was attending his flock. The cave was full of gold bunion. It was one of the biggest gold strikes in all of Egypt.

The Herdsman who left his homeland to find his wealth forgot to check his own backyard for riches. So he gave up all he owned, including his life, to look for something he already had in his grasp.

We all have great wealth in our possession. We often forget to check our backyards for it. Learn to recognize the riches you already have in your possession.

The First Day

• • • • •

Today is the first day of the rest of your life. Most of us have heard this axiom before; but have we really thought about what it actually means. Today we can begin in an entirely new direction, if we choose to do so. We can shoot upward, downwards or even sideways. The choice is ours. Since this is the first day of the rest of your life, the choices you make will greatly influence the next days of your life.

Make this day count for you and it will have a domino effect on your future days. Make it the best day ever. Whatever your schedule might be today, you can make it a memorable day. A day that will be the foundation of all succeeding days. Your day will be as positive and exciting as you allow it to be. Permit this first day of the rest of your life to become one of your best days ever. Set out to make it one you will always remember. The choice is yours!

You Have the Talent

• • • • •

Test your abilities every now and then. Don't let others tell you what you can or cannot achieve. Find out for yourself. You'll never truly know your own capability until you personally test the waters.

Be yourself as you pursue your goals. Find out where your talents are and how you can utilize them to help you achieve your very best. Once you discover your talents – and we all have them – work to develop your skills in that specific area.

If you're a cement finisher, work to be the very best cement finisher in your area, then the very best in your state, then the very best in the nation. Whatever your field, there is a little difference in being the very best or being average, and that little difference is ATTITUDE. The best have learned to believe in their inert abilities and to let nothing stand in the way of their success. They give that extra effort when things get a little tough. They come to the playing field of life to win.

We have all the necessary talent to excel within us. However, the onus is upon us to develop those talents. When we work relentlessly to excel – we excel.

A Season for Change

• • • • •

The fall of the year can be a great time to implement change. The temperature is dropping a few degrees. Leaves are falling from the trees. Students are back in the classrooms and the squirrels are going about the serious business of gathering their winter food supply.

These are natural occurrences that take place every year. Seasonal changes are natures way of renewing itself. Initiating a personal change can be your way of renewing yourself. Everyday we have the opportunity to enact change. We do not have to await the changes in the seasons to initiate a change in our lives. But, just as nature creates the opportunity to revise itself, by changing seasons, we can create an opportunity to renew ourselves by following nature's lead and periodically implementing any positive change in our behavior.

Therefore, as the seasons change, four times a year, why not take this opportunity to reflect on your lifes ambitions and make the adjustments that will help you stay on track or even create new tracks on your way to success.

It's Your Choice

• • • • •

We begin everyday with a choice. What we chose to do or say will determine the level of success in our day and for everything that our day holds. We can choose to tackle the challenges of our day with the belief that we will excel at every endeavor. Or, we can choose not to make a choice regarding the outcome of any event that our day presents to us.

Choosing to believe that we will excel at every encounter we meet is just as easy as choosing to believe that today's challenges are too gigantic for us. If we choose to believe that we will not be successful at today's challenges then we have lost much of the battle before we start.

By thinking that we will not be successful, we place all of our inner talents on hold. But on the other hand, if we tell ourselves that we will excel, we release all of our inner strengths and alert them to prepare for the task that stands ahead. We must make sure that we have chosen to believe that we can successfully meet any challenge we encounter before we attempt to overcome that challenge. This will help to ensure your success.

Computer Mind

• • • • •

A computer is the most complex piece of machinery that man has created. In recent years it has become the most important non–living object in the world. The computer is used to design automobiles and airplanes. It is used to assist surgeons in highly technical brain surgery. Without it man could not efficiently conduct space exploration or travel. The computer allows scientists to split atoms. It allows farmers to more effectively produce crops – worldwide. Wall Street would stop cold without computers.

Computers are by far the most complex and brilliant items made by man, however, the most sophisticated computer cannot compare with the complexity of the human mind. Your mind is capable of achieving feats that far exceed the talents of any machine. Scientists believe that we only use approximately ten percent of our total brain capacity. Yet, we were able to create computers and we constantly find ways to improve upon them. Our brain does not have an on/off switch. It constantly works to solve any problems put before it.

If you program your mind to solve problems, it will solve them for you every time. Like a computer your mind does require a password. The universal password for the mind is "I CAN" – (That's I CAN.) Use it to get where you want to go.

The Playing Field Of Life

• • • • •

We can be in the game of life each and every day and have those things in life that we want most greet us on the playing field of life. There's no need to observe from a seat in the stand, even if it is a front row seat.

There is a place on the field reserved for anyone who wants it. The only thing we need to do is run onto the field and take our positions. We can be the captain, the coach, the referee or the quarterback. The choice is ours, however, the game will not wait for us. We must be decisive about the role we want to play and work to fulfill that role.

If we play our parts well, in the game of life, the rewards will come streaking towards us. The more efficient we are at executing this most rewarding game, the greater the rewards. Prepare well, practice hard, and be ready to take your position as the star in today's game. Remember, don't settle for a seat in the stands when you can be on the playing field of life, taking charge of the game.

Lets Get Lucky

• • • • •

Do you ever wonder why some people appear luckier than others. Why some people always seem to have it their way (even without going to Burger King). They just win all the time or at least most of the time.

Perhaps those people understand luck or have an understanding of how luck can be controlled. Now, controlling luck may seem like a contradictory statement; however, you can control your luck when you understand its total definition. Webster's Dictionary defines luck as: prospering or succeeding through chance. Many highly successful people define luck as the event that occurs when opportunity meets preparation.

If an opportunity comes along and you're not prepared to accept it, you will lose the opportunity. Conversely, when an opportunity comes along and you're well prepared for it, you will be the luckiest guy in town. When your opportunity meets with your preparation you'll win over and over again. The lucky people are those who plan ahead and prepare to succeed. Why not get lucky – prepare yourself for the opportunities that are advancing in your direction at this very moment.

Get Pumped Up

• • • • •

It's great to be pumped up everyday. We can get more out of life when we're excited about life. We all know that a bicycle with a flat tire will not move as smoothly or as quickly as one with perfectly inflated tires. Likewise, we do not function as well when our minds are under inflated or when we are psychologically down.

If the tire on our bicycle needed air, we would place air in the tire before we put the bike to use. The same should hold true for our minds. Sometimes it is necessary to pump up our minds so that we can travel through the day with greater ease and efficiency.

There are literally hundreds of ways to pump ourselves up. We can read motivational materials, we can listen to inspirational tapes, we can repeat positive affirmations like: "I'm feeling better already." Or, we can seek out spiritually uplifting messages. Whatever you decide to do, give it a chance to work for you. Inflate your mind with positiveness as frequently as you can. Give It A Try! Then, watch for the change in your day, the change in your week and the change in your life. Get Pumped Up–Today.

The Greater the Risk the Greater the Return

•   •   •   •   •

All of us take risk on a daily basis. Every time we leave our homes we take a risk. No one knows what the day might bring. The risk we take naturally like walking down a flight of stairs, turning on a gas stove or even getting out of bed are normally not very dangerous. We do them so frequently we hardly consider them risks. However, they are risks, nonetheless.

Risk taking can be great for our personal or professional growth, just as the lack of taking risk can stifle our growth. As we have learned to accept low level risk, taking as a part of our daily routine, we should also learn to periodically incorporate greater risk taking in our lives. The general rule of thumb about risk taking is: The greater the risk, the greater the possible gain should be. A key to risk taking is avoiding risks that have a high possibility of leaving you with far less than what you started with and concentrating on taking risks that have a fair to good chance of succeeding.

Take more risks in all areas of your life. It can help you personally, professionally and of course financially. Risk taking can be fun. Try It!

Our Untapped Talent

• • • • •

Our success or failure in life depends not so much on what happens to us, but on how we handle what happens to us. Perhaps you have heard the story about the woman who's car flipped on a slippery road and pinned her infant son beneath it. The car weighed 3700 pounds, but it was no match for her love for her son. She raised the car using every ounce of muscle she possessed and her son crawled to safety. To look at her frail body you would think she would have trouble lifting 25 pounds off the ground, but when it came to a life or death situation, her mind gave her body the strength of ten strong men.

This is just one story, out of thousands, where remarkable feats were performed by average human beings. There are literally countless numbers of people who have turned severe adversities into raving successes. They all have learned to concentrate, not on their weakness, but on developing the necessary strength to meet an overbearing situation.

All of us have untapped talents within us. If there is something that is standing in the way of your progress, concentrate on going over it, around it or right through it, if necessary. Whatever you do, don't let a negative situation control you. Let the positiveness in your mind control it.

You Have Great Talent Within You

• • • • •

Did you know that nature has provided all earthly beings with everything that is essential for survival. Eagles fly through the air with the greatest of ease with wings that span up to six feet in length and with eyes that have the ability to sight prey from over a mile away. The cheetah is one of the fastest animals on earth. Traveling over 60 miles per hour they are able to change direction in a split second during a chase.

Man has not been excluded from natures kindness, we are designed to achieve our objective with ease and efficiency. When we relax and let the natural abilities that we possess intuitively guide us, we'll find that we have everything necessary for success firmly inside us. We must trust our instincts and just as the eagle and the cheetah, we can also soar to meet our objectives in life with the utmost precision. We have all the talents necessary for great achievements. Nature has designed us for success so let your natural talents work for you. Don't question your ability – Just Do It.

Firm Foundations

• • • • •

Most of our houses are built on firm foundations. Without a solid foundation the chances of long term existence is always in jeopardy. The first inkling of inclement weather can destroy all of the work sitting on a weak foundation. It's essential that investments as significant as our homes be built to weather the harshest storms.

Just as your house should be built on a solid foundation your life should also be built on solid ground. Life is the most precious possession each of us holds. Developing it on shaky ground is very risky business. A foundation of solid concrete several feet thick holds a house firmly intact. A firm positive mental attitude is a great foundation for anyone's life. It is just like three feet of solid concrete beneath a house, it will withstand most any storm.

We should work to ensure that our positive mental foundations are strong. Strong enough to meet the storms that sometimes cross our paths. Why not start building your positive mental foundation today! You'll be glad you did!

Just Don't Give In

• • • • •

We all know that pursing a new direction in life can be very painful and frustrating at times. The growth process is often full of hardship especially when we are trying to accomplish something new or unfamiliar to us. Fortunately, the pain and hardship we sometimes feel whenever we are starting new ventures is usually just temporary. The pleasure, as a result of our arduous work, will soon follow.

So, if there is some pain when you are experiencing a change or embarking upon a territory, you can be sure that you're making progress. Because, if there's no pain there is often no gain. I'm sure you have heard it said many times before: "NO PAIN NO GAIN."

The frustration we may experience is often necessary as we break old barriers. If we endure this temporary discomfort, the rewards can be limitless. Just don't give in, even if rough roads and hardships appear along the way. When we continue to move forward we will eventually, without exception, reach our destinations.

The Positive Thought

•　•　•　•　•

Did you know it's a proven scientific fact that the human mind cannot hold two opposing thoughts at the same time. One of these thoughts must leave before the other can enter. If this is the case then we can combat any negative self destructive thought as soon as it appears by replacing it with a positive self assuring thought.

Try this exercise. As soon as a thought you would consider negative, enters your mind replace it with the exact opposite positive thought. Without exception, every negative thought can be replaced by a positive thought. For example: When we first encounter a challenging situation we may automatically think that we cannot handle it. This thought itself can actually hinder our attempts to tame the situation. However, its positive counterpart; which is: "I can handle it," can significantly improve the situation.

Repeating this new thought over and over will not only remove the negative thought, it will reinforce the positive thought. Try replacing all negative thoughts with positive ones. The positive thought will lead you to a positive outcome, every time.

Have a Personal Mission Statement

• • • • •

Have you ever wondered about your mission in life. You know, the things you want to achieve in life. You may want to be the best possible mother your children can have. You may want to be the very best father that you can be. Your mission may be to become a top surgeon or a highly respected teacher or a great wife or husband.

Whatever your mission keep it close to you; write your mission on paper and read it daily. Make it as special as possible to you. Almost all major corporations have a mission statement. It helps to keep them focused and on track as they move towards their goals and objectives. It can do the same for you.

If you're lost in the middle of the woods, a compass can keep you from going in the wrong direction. The same holds true for your mission statement. It will keep you going in the right direction. Choose your mission and focus on it. Work hard to become closer to it. Eventually, you'll find yourself living that mission to the fullest extent possible.

It's Mutually Beneficial

• • • • •

Throughout my professional career I have been fortunate enough to meet and interact with many of what most of us would consider highly successful people. The one thing I found that all of these individuals had in common was an understanding of the importance of helping others.

Someone once said, "If you want to be successful, do what successful people do." This has always made good sense to me. Successful people consistently find time to help others. As a matter of fact, most seem to have a history of helping people. We may or may not find immediate gratification in helping our fellow human beings, but you can be sure that there is long-term satisfaction in it.

A certain percentage of those that you help, will never forget your efforts, and will always support you whenever they can. Furthermore, your kindness will make your community a better place to live, work and prosper. Think about it this way, if everyone helped everyone else, it would be easier for all of us to succeed. Help someone today – It's mutually beneficial.

A Competitive Spirit Will Bring Out The Best In You

• • • • •

Throughout our endeavors in life there will be competition. Whenever the competition is good we must become better if we want to stand out from the crowd. Fortunately, our society is built upon competition. As toddlers, we compete for our mother's attention, as kids in school we compete for our teachers approval, as adults we compete for jobs, promotions, and a host of other things.

Competition is not a stranger to us. It's a way of life and healthy competition can be great for everyone. It can help us focus on our goals and it can bring the very best performance out of us.

Whenever our competitors perform well we often find ourselves performing better to meet the challenge of staying in the game. So, when the competition is good, prepare yourself to meet the challenge. Dig down deep for that inner strength that will help you excel. Let your competitive spirit bring out the best of your talents and skills. You'll find yourself reaching new heights and breaking new ground when you allow your natural competitive spirit to work in a positive manner.

Pure Faith

•   •   •   •   •

Sometimes we just have to have faith. Faith is having belief in something and not letting go of that belief regardless of how horrific a situation might appear. When things become real tough our faith is receiving its greatest challenge. Having total faith is believing even when things look nearly impossible. Sometimes we must totally commit ourselves to the outcome we want to see happen before we do anything else.

Perhaps you want to return to school after being out for several years. Or, perhaps you would like to apply for a new position at work. But, maybe you feel you don't have the time to dedicate to night school or maybe you feel others will have a better chance of getting that new position. This is where faith can help. By having total and complete faith in ourselves and our abilities, we are taking one of the first and most important steps in reaching our desires. Without faith in the outcome, it can be very difficult to move smoothly towards your goals. However, when you have faith in you – you can achieve absolutely, positively, unconditionally everything you believe you can achieve. May your life be full of faith!

The Most Important Element

• • • • •

What is the single most important element in a persons quest for greater achievement in life? Well, that single element is, without a doubt, attitude. Have you ever wondered why some people always appear to have an easier time achieving results than others? Believe it or not, their attitude towards what they have to do has a tremendous and total impact on the outcome of their work.

Over the years, countless achievement experts, writers and speakers, have pointed out that achieving success is 90 percent attitude. Your attitude toward whatever you want to achieve will leave an indelible print on your work. It's nearly impossible to find a book, in print, on achievement that does not spend at least a chapter on the importance of attitude.

It's crucial that our attitudes are consistent with what we want to occur. If we want a positive outcome, from whatever we attempt, we must input a positive attitude before we even begin. Attitude is number one!

Making A Positive Change

• • • • •

Are you making a change in your life? Making a change can of course bring greater happiness and fulfillment into our lives. However, as easy as this may sound most of us find personal change hard to come by.

Changing often means throwing away the old and accepting the new - getting rid of bad unwanted habits and creating new more desirable ones. It's not always easy to remove unwanted habits even if you know they're not good for you; and it's not easy accepting new habits even if they are good for you.

To make a positive change we must sometimes destroy the old habits, no matter how painful that might be. And, we must also practice incorporating new habits, no matter how uncomfortable that process might be initially.

Consider making the changes that will improve your progress in life. You'll be glad you did!

A Loss Is Not A Loss

• • • • •

Did you know that there are valuable lessons that can be learned when we lose a battle, contest, game or position.

Often we are so afraid of losing that we will do anything to avoid it. And when it happens we frequently try to forget everything that has occurred. We shove all thoughts of our loss into a closet, lock the door and throw away the key.

Well in every loss there is much to be learned. First of all, we have discovered what will not work for us. We have also learned more about our strengths and weaknesses, as well as the strengths and weaknesses of our competition. Losses are rarely permanent situations. They are normally just temporary set-backs. If you view it in this manner, your loss is not really a loss, it's a tremendous gain for you.

Nurture Your Mind

• • • • •

I want to share a unique kind of gardening with you. That unique kind of gardening is the type of gardening our minds require. Our minds will only produce the out–growth of what we plant in it.

We can produce flowers or weeds, the choice is ours. Of course, if we plant beautiful neatly arranged thoughts and water them with reinforcement everyday; when it's time for the harvest, we will have an abundance of positive organized thoughts, ready to help us meet every challenge.

On the other hand, if we let the weeds infiltrate the garden of our mind, or neglect to nurture it with progressive thoughts daily, we'll smother our ability to adequately meet our daily challenges.

Plant powerful, progressive thoughts in your mind and rein-force them with positiveness everyday. Then, get prepared to use your well nurtured mind to take you anywhere you choose to go in life. Feed and nurture the garden in your mind.

Full Attention And Commitment

• • • • •

Did you know that very few things will not yield to us when we give them our full attention and commitment.

Perhaps you have heard about the one– legged man who ran across his entire country after being told by doctors that he would never be able to walk again, or the one–armed professional baseball pitcher who struck out scores of batters during his career. He was told that he would never make the team, however, the team came to depend on him for a winning season. Both of these individuals certainly beat the odds. But, it was not without their full attention and commitment to the task at hand.

If we give an assignment or task 100 percent of our effort and seek only success we'll find success every time. Whatever your objectives are in life, give them your full attention and commitment. Great feats will bow to your command and nothing will keep you from reaching your dreams.

Overall Potential Is Unlimited

• • • • •

Have you ever assessed your overall potential? Have you ever tried to determine what your limits really are? Very few of us push ourselves to our full potential. As a matter of record, it's a proven fact that humans generally operate far below their optimal ability.

Working at or near 100 percent of our potential, 100 percent of the time, would probably put our systems on overload. Burnout would soon follow. However, pushing yourself occasionally to do the best that you can do, will gradually increase your overall level of production no matter what your goals might be.

If you get accustomed to pushing yourself just a little beyond what you normally do, you'll start to increase your level of achievement. Each time you increase your level of achievement you increase your overall potential. Of course, your overall potential is unlimited.

Your Secret Guide

• • • • •

Have you ever thought about finding a mentor to help you achieve your objectives in life. Nine times out of ten someone else has walked down at least a portion of the path that you intend to travel. If this is the case, that person might know where the hazards are located and where the rewards can be found.

Anyone trying to accomplish something worthwhile should find a mentor. A mentor can keep you going in the right direction. He can open locked doors and most importantly he can keep you focused on your overall objectives. You probably have experts in your field or the field you want to pursue. Just ask one of them if they will help you occasionally. I'll bet you they'll say yes every time.

Don't go at it alone when you have your own personal guide to success. Find your mentor! He's waiting to assist you!

Jump Right In Head First

• • • • •

Do you remember trying to get into a swimming pool that was full of cold water? Many times we put our feet in first, just to feel how cold it is. Then we might jump in where the water is only up to our waist. We're afraid to go all the way in because it's just too cold, and we're also not sure what to do next. On one hand, we want to stay in and have some fun, but, on the other hand we want to get out because our bodies have not adjusted to the cold temperature.

So, we jump up and down splashing just a little water on us at a time hoping to gradually become adjusted to the cold. Of course, all of this aggravation could have been avoided, if we had just jumped straight into the pool. In a matter of seconds we would adjust to the temperature of the water.

Life's challenges are just like a cold swimming pool. Frequently, we have to jump right in and tackle them. Moving too cautiously can prolong the discomfort. Sometimes you just have to dive in head first and be confident that everything will be okay. Tackle your problems, don't let them tackle you.

Law Of Nature

• • • • •

You know, it's just a simple law of nature. You cannot hit any object above which you are aiming. If you're shooting for the ground you cannot hit the tree tops.

In life you've got to aim high. If you're making plans make big ones. Aim for targets that will reap great rewards for you. Wherever you aim you will probably hit the target ... or something below it. Its very unlikely you'll hit anything above your sights.

If you really want to hit the tree tops, why not aim for the stars. If you miss the stars, you just might hit those tree tops. Either way, you'll still be far above the ground.

We can seek anything we choose in life, however, whatever we choose to aim for will determine what we ultimately hit.

Keep your sights high and you'll hit the more exciting targets.

I Thank God For Problems

• • • • •

You know I have learned to thank God for problems. If none of us had any problems I wonder where we would be.

Napoleon Hill a world renowned Motivational speaker tells a story of how a man ran up to him on Fifth Avenue, in New York City, grabbed him by the lapels and demanded his help. The man had heard of Mr. Hill's work and he thought Hill could solve all of his problems.

Mr. Hill told the man if he would let him go, he would show him a place where no one has any problems, to speak of. The man released him and asked how far was it to this place. Hill replied "About two blocks away." Then he walked the man to a graveyard nearby and said "no one here has a problem." Problems are a natural part of life. Every living person has them. Solving them builds our character and makes us stronger people. I thank God I'm alive to tackle any "problem" that comes my way.

The Proper Perspective

• • • • •

Success and failure are both very natural parts of life. Without failure there cannot be success. Believe it or not, everyone fails. As a matter of fact, successful people often fail a lot more than the average person. Therefore, we should not throw in the towel when we don't meet our objectives the first few times we attempt them. Successful individuals review their failures then make whatever adjustments are necessary and try again. Facing failure is a natural part of finding success. Thomas Edison failed over one thousand times before he discovered the incandescent light.

If you adopt this logic, you'll keep undesirable events in their proper perspective. Success and failure are both very normal parts of life. We must learn to accept them both.

Focus On The Positive

• • • • •

All of our focus should be on the things we want to see develop in our lives. Energy wasted thinking about what we don't want can only slow us down.

Hank Aaron is the greatest homerun hitter of all time. He, like many others, focused on the record breaking 755 homeruns he hit. You rarely heard about the many times he struck out before he hit all of those homeruns.

Like most great hitters, he struck out more than the average players. However, his focus was on hitting homeruns and the rest is history. Of course, if he had focused on striking out, the history books would be telling a different story.

If you can, spend all of your energy focused on what you want to occur. Forget the negative thoughts. They will only slow you down. Focus on the positive outcome and in time you will see the results.

Expect The Best

· · · · ·

Did you know that everything we accomplish in life is a result of conditioning. When we condition ourselves to expect the best from whatever we choose to do we increase our chances for higher achievement.

We normally deliver to ourselves, whatever we expect from ourselves. That's why it is crucial for us to always think in terms of what we want to accomplish, and, not in terms of what we don't want to occur.

High expectations often leads to high results. Just as low expectations often lead to low results. If we condition ourselves to truly expect the very best, from all situations, then our very best will surface over and over again.

Condition yourself to expect the best in all that you do then work to bring the exciting results to your door.

Clear Skies Ahead

• • • • •

Does your "Boat of Life" have a rudder on it? All boats need some sort of steering device. A rudder on a boat is like a steering wheel in a car. Without it we have no control over where we're going.

In life, our conscious mind is our rudder. The thoughts we hold control what we do and where we go. A boat with no rudder will float aimlessly. It will be at the whim of any hazards that might appear. The same is true for us humans, without firm control of our thoughts we float aimlessly in life.

But, like a boat with a rudder, we can guide ourselves to all of those things that are important to us. We have the power to steer our thoughts in any direction we choose. There are clear skies ahead of us and we have the power to adjust our rudder to sail for the calm waters. We can do this simply by focusing on positive thoughts.

Like A Dedicated Soldier

• • • • •

Did you know that whatever we say and believe becomes a reality for us. Whenever we say I can't do something, we place every one of our 14 billion brain cells on alert. We have ordered them to avoid success. Success has been placed on hold. Instead of working to solve a problem for us, our brain is now working to ensure that we can't solve the problem.

The brain operates on a subconscious level. It only carries out the orders that we give it. It is like a dedicated soldier, it will work diligently to carry out your command. We must be very careful about what we say or think.

If we say we can't, our brain will work to make this a reality. This is why negative thoughts or comments can be very damaging to us. On the other hand, when we say, I can, our 14 billion brain cells work to make this a reality. Only say and think about what you really want to see happen in your life.

Make It Appear In Your Mind First

• • • • •

Did you know that you can be the best! You can excel at work, at home or at school. Someone has to be the best and that someone can be you. At whatever you do, see yourself doing it well. Close your eyes and visualize yourself excelling. See your boss giving you that plaque saying #1 achiever.

Visualize your co-workers happily slapping you on the back. They're smiling and saying how great you are. Now see yourself doing a fantastic job. Imagine your results being well beyond what was expected of you. And don't forget to visualize your boss handing you that bonus check, or offering you a promotion.

Take a few minutes each day to relax and see yourself getting all the things you want. Make it appear in your mind first. This is one of the critical steps toward achieving excellence.

Face Your Fears

• • • • •

Do you want to overcome your fears? Are your fears holding you back, or stopping you from doing something you need to do? We must face our fears, no matter how difficult that may be.

Do what you fear the most! And, do it often. The more frequently we tackle our fears; the more accustomed we'll become to the things that we fear. Once we become accustomed to them the fear will go away.

We usually fear the unknown. Applying for a new position, taking an exam, or for some, just leaving the house can be fearful. Face your fears head on! You'll find out that you are tougher than they are.

Fear normally alerts us to an upcoming challenge. It helps us to prepare for whatever may come our way. Don't turn away. Face fear frequently, and you'll meet or beat the challenge.

A Great Champion

• • • • •

Lets talk about a great champion. Over and over again we hear about the deeds of great champions. In the fall of 1993 the big and lovable George Foreman, a boxing legend, defeated his opponent Michael Moore. According to all accounts, he was losing the match until one of his punches startled the world. To the amazement of many, George Foreman knocked out Michael Moore.

He, like many other great champions, came to the ring to win. The odds were way against him. But, to the heart of a champion, the odds mean very little. According to most, he was over weight, over aged and over matched. However, big George had a big heart. And loosing wasn't a part of his plan.

He came to the game to win. After the bout, he said he always knew he could become champion again. The lovable George Foreman's dream became a reality. No matter what our circumstances, each of us is a champion. If you keep swinging you'll also deliver a knock–out blow, that will startle the world.

Meeting Highly Effective People

• • • • •

Did you know that the people you meet, and interact with, can completely change your life? Meeting highly effective people and learning their secrets will definitely enhance your personal growth.

We never stop learning and we learn most from those with which we interact. The more we meet and converse with highly effective people, the greater our personal possibility for growth and development.

Formulate a group of questions that you would like to ask someone very successful. Make your questions straight forward and to the point. Then, identify those persons from whom you can learn. You might choose someone in your workplace, school, church or any other setting. It may or may not be someone you are familiar with. Talk to as many people as you can.

You'll be surprised at the number of folks that will be absolutely honored to share their positive experiences with you. They will help you find the right track for your success, and you might even make a few new friends along with way.

Time And Productive Results

• • • • •

What is one of the most precious commodities each of us holds? Well, the precious commodity I'm thinking of is TIME. Just about everything we do is contingent upon time. Time will not adjust itself for any man. No matter what we are doing, time will always continue to move forward.

Each one of us is allotted so much time on earth, we should allocate it to the best possible usage. The more time we spend on productive pursuits, the quicker we'll reach our goals.

Use the time wisely. Spend a good portion of it making your dream become a reality. If you can, stay away from those things that will drain this precious commodity, and give you little in return.

If necessary, force yourself toward productive activity as frequently as you can and do as much of that activity as you possibly can. Let time work for you. Your efforts will render you great success.

Plan Your Way To A More Productive Day

• • • • •

If you plan your way, you'll have a much more productive day! Only 3 percent of Americans write down their goals. That means 97 percent of us rely on our memory to do what we have to do each day. Most of us have trouble remembering what we had for lunch two days ago. Yet, we try to remember everything we need to do 24 hours a day, seven days a week.

One of the most productive things we can do each morning is to write down our goals for the day. If we really want to be ahead of the game we can make a list the night before.

We get more done when we go after our goals in an organized fashion. If you write them down you won't forget them. If you don't forget them that eliminates an excuse for not doing them. Make a list and refer to it throughout the day. You'll become a step closer to mega achievements.

Just Do It

• • • • •

Is there anything that you don't like about your life? Are there somethings about yourself you would like to improve or change? Well I have good news for you!

You can change your life starting today. You can have every positive attribute you have always wanted, and you can do it now. You don't have to be the same person you've always been. Today you can become a new person. Just decide to do it!

Yes, all you have to do is decide to change. Tell your old self goodbye and welcome the new you to town. Moreover, creating a new you can be fun. Give yourself all of the positive attributes you can think of. Walk a little faster. Talk a little louder, and smile a little longer. Think positive thoughts and start feeling more confident. At this very moment you can become that happy go lucky, free spirited soul you've always wanted to be. All you have to do is just do it!

Any Time You Choose Too

• • • • •

You know you can start bringing greater improvements to all parts of your life anytime you choose to do so. You can initiate a positive change today, or you can wait two years from now to start.

Unfortunately, waiting two years will prolong the rewards you'll get from making a positive or progressive change. Most of us would rather initiate a change sooner than later. And of course the benefits of change will come sooner when we act sooner.

Two years from now you will be the same person you are today except for the books you read, the people you meet and all the other information you choose to gather and internalize.

If we want to grow we must meet positive people, and read inspiring books, and seek out as much positive information as we possibly can.

I'm sure you'll agree, there is no better time than today to start bringing greater benefits your way.

Alter Your Efforts

• • • • •

As you probably know most people would love to increase their annual income. There could be no better time to plan a financial strategy than now. That is if you haven't done so already.

Right now is not too soon to develop a winning plan for the remainder of this year or next year. Think of the head start you'll have if you start planning now. As the saying goes "you'll hit the ground running."

If you take this attitude, you can make some serious gains in the near future. Reflect on what you have been doing to earn funds. Then think about a few ways you can alter your efforts. Perhaps you're interested in starting a part–time home business. It can be fun and very profitable. Of course, this is just one of many income earning ideas. No matter what you do if you start planning now, this year can be your best year ever.

Past Successes

• • • • •

Did you know that the successes of your past can be of great help to you. All of us need reinforcement and reassurance. Our past experiences can give us that extra push whenever we need it.

Our brain is a warehouse of knowledge. In that warehouse, there is an arsenal of great memories that can inspire us. Whenever you are feeling a little down, or have a pressing challenge, recall one of your past successes. Think about how nice that success made you feel.

You might have written an "A" paper in school, or ran your first mile, or helped someone to solve a problem. Whatever that success was, think about what it did for you and others. If you can, recall your past successes just before you attempt new challenges. You will find that your previous successes have already laid the ground work for any current challenges. Think about your past successes often, no matter how small or large they might have been. Your mind has retained them for a reason.

Most Criticism Is Beneficial

• • • • •

Criticism from others can be the best possible source of information to help us identify our weaknesses. Be like a Rhino with tough skin when it comes to personal criticism. Just don't take it too personal. You can use it to improve certain aspects of your life.

You'll know when the criticism is relayed to you in a harmful way and you'll know when its given to you in a loving way. Some of us welcome criticism with open arms, and some of us take it as if we have been hit with a ton of bricks.

Even criticism given you in a deliberately harmful way can benefit you if you can gather the strength to overlook the harmful intent. Look for the positive in what was said. Use that to your benefit. Now that deliberately harmful intent is now deliberately helpful. Remember, any criticism issued to you with harmful intent can be transformed into something helpful.

Just Ordinary People Doing Extraordinary Things

• • • • •

Ordinary people just like you and I are doing extraordinary things all over the world. In England, years ago, four ordinary guys got together and started playing music. Two years later those four ordinary guys were known as the Beatles and their songs were played all over the globe.

Several decades ago, a seemingly ordinary young man was jailed for standing up against the crimes of his country. After countless years in jail, he was released. Shortly after his release, Nelson Mandella was elected president of his nation. Not far from home, an ordinary college student hoped to inspire the world with his words. Today you can hardly find a country where Billy Graham hasn't spoken and inspired thousands of people.

In Atlanta, a king was born to ordinary parents. Of course he was just an ordinary guy named King until he had a dream. Now Martin Luther King Jr. is among the extraordinary. Ordinary people just like you and I are doing extraordinary things all over the world. We all start off ordinary until we decide to do something extraordinary.

A Whole New You

• • • • •

Did you know that according to scientists, every cell in our body changes about every eleven months? That means you are truly not the same person you were a year ago.

To some of us, this can be bad news. We may feel one-hundred and one percent satisfied with who we are and believe there is no room for improvement. But, to the vast majority of us, this can be some of the best news ever.

Once a year, nature takes away the old and creates the new. Just like the change in our physical self, we can change our mental self. The greater news is we don't have to wait eleven months to renew or improve our mental well- being. We can Do-it-Now! List five positive attributes you would like to incorporate in your life. Everyday religiously study and work on achieving those attributes. If you work diligently, before you know it, those attributes will become your attributes. You'll become a new person physically as well as mentally.

Deposits And Withdrawals

• • • • •

You know, everything we achieve in life is a direct reflection of what we put into life. The more effort we put in, the greater the rewards are for us.

I constantly meet with and read about people who extend above and beyond the norm to achieve high levels of success. They start their work day before most of us. They take shorter lunch breaks. They read during their work breaks and they constantly push themselves toward success.

These people are determined to improve their lives. Nothing will stand in their way. They want more out of life and are willing to work for it. They understand the law of give and take. You can't take out what you haven't put in.

Absolutely everything we achieve in life is relative to our efforts. The more we perform, the more we will achieve. It's really simple! If we want more than average out of life, we have to put more than average into life.

A Few Minutes
To Concentrate

• • • • •

Focusing on our goals can bring all of our desires to reality. When we totally focus on what we want to achieve and let nothing steer us astray, we'll bring our desires home, time and time again.

Focusing is simply selecting what you want, then concentrating on bringing that to you. Perhaps you want a new car, a house or a college degree. It may be a position at work that you desire or a mate to share your life with. Focusing can bring anything to anyone. Of course, as you focus you must work towards your objectives. Unfortunately, distractions will take you away from your goals. However, you can keep yourself on track by focusing on your target.

If you find your dreams slipping away just buckle down and pull them back to you. If need be, take a few minutes everyday to concentrate on nothing but your goals and then work diligently to make them your reality.

Desire It
More Than Anything

• • • • •

I'd like to share with you a story about a young man who was seeking success. It occurred years ago in a distant land. This young man asked a wise man how he could find success. The wise man replied: "Follow me". He took the boy to a pit full of snakes and pushed the boy in. The boy scrambled out of the pit almost as fast as he fell in. When the boy reached safety the old man asked him, "What did you want most when you were in the snake pit?" The boy said, "I wanted to get out". The wise old man said to him, "When you want success as much as you wanted to get out of that pit, success will be yours."

Success often comes to those who desire it most. Make sure you have a strong desire to achieve your objectives in life. Your level of desire will determine your level of achievement.

Your Subconscious State Of Being

• • • • •

Did you know that your subconscious mind works for you twenty-four hours a day, seven days a week. Your subconscious mind never rests. It controls everything we do physically and mentally. Our heart rate, breathing and thoughts, are all controlled by the subconscious. If our subconscious stopped working, we would cease to exist. Therefore, its important that we keep our inner self strong. We must feed our subconscious positive information. We must feed it thoughts that will help it help us.

There are documented stories of meditation specialists who lowered their heart rate to a near stop. They learned to effectively tap into their subconscious state. From there they controlled their physical state.

Our mental condition controls what we achieve in life, and we can control our mental condition. Just feed it positive information. That is, information that's consistent with what you want to achieve. If you can, spend at least 10-minutes a day actively feeding your subconscious mind progressive thoughts.

Stay Focused
On Your Dreams

•　　•　　•　　•　　•

You know, millions of great ideas have been lost due to a lack of focus. Sadly, many of us have forgotten or discarded great ideas because we forgot to stay focused on them, or we were distracted by something less important than our ideas.

Once you have an idea, challenge yourself to keep focused on it. We know distractions are all around us. Whenever we have something positive going on, distractions seem to come out of the woodwork. Your friends call more frequently. You'll get a new assignment at work. Or, your children will require more attention than usual.

But, regardless of the distractions, if you want to see your dreams become a reality, force yourself to stay focused. Dedicate a period of time that is exclusively for your dreams. Don't take calls. Make arrangements for your kids. Put your other work aside. Remember, this is "Your Dream" we're talking about! When we stay focused day after day, we'll meet any challenge that comes our way.

Outside The Zone

•　•　•　•　•

Did you know that most of the personal growth in our lives normally occurs outside of our comfort zone. Our comfort zone is where we have been conditioned to remain in life mostly because it's comfortable to us and requires little personal fortitude.

When we desire to improve, or accomplish more in life, we must often move out of our comfort zone. For most of us this is very difficult to do. However, this is one of the most rewarding moves we can make for our personal development.

Moving out of our comfort zone means doing things we normally wouldn't do. For example, we could stop by our supervisor's office, just to wish him well, or we could send our clients birthday cards. We could get up earlier or work later. Any progressive change we make outside our comfort zone will elevate our personal and professional development.

Find progressive activities outside your comfort zone and do them regularly. It might be difficult at first, but remember your personal and professional growth depends upon it.

You're The Star

• • • • •

Did you know that you are the producer, director and the star of your life. The average person controls more than 90 percent of what happens in their life. We have more influence on the outcome of our lives than anyone or anything else.

As we walk through life, we determine what type of star we're going to become. We can dance in a Broadway Show; ride a horse into the sunset on the big screen in Hollywood or become a Wall Street corporate executive. We can become a successful homemaker or a premier educator. The choices in life are endless.

But, just like any big star, we certainly have to work hard and smart to become successful. There is simply no suitable replacement for work. Every successful individual knows the value of work. And, when we choose hard work we have chosen the path to success.

Everybody is the star of their own life. What type of star we become depends solely on the choices we make. As producer, director, and star of your life you can choose the great roles to play.

You're The Expert

• • • • •

Do you ever feel like you're in a rut? Each day is the same, day in and day out. You would just like to escape from it all.

Well there's good news. No, I mean great news! We can learn anything we want to learn and achieve anything we want to achieve. You can become an expert at anything you choose. Just find an interest that you would like to develop. Perhaps you're interested in Graphic Design, Egyptian Art or Space Exploration.

Whatever your interest, learn as much as there is to know about that subject. The library is inundated with free information. Other experts are only a phone call away. You can find a workshop or seminar on just about any subject. Once you know all there is to know, you become the expert. Employers are always looking for experts and, of course, many experts become self–employed.

Webster's dictionary defines an expert as: one who has acquired special skill or knowledge in a particular subject. You certainly can be the expert. Just choose what type of expert you want to become, then, learn your way to a better day.

Every One Of Us Is Born Great

• • • • •

Have you ever wondered why some people achieve greatness while others meander about in hopelessness. Well, the answer is on the inside of each of us.

People all over the world have achieved greatness. Regardless of economic background or environmental conditioning; greatness will always shine through.

I guess you can say it's something special that each one of us has inside. Every one of us is born great. We just have to pull that greatness out one day at a time.

The hopeless have stopped pulling–out their greatness. They have sold out, closed shop and moved away. Ironically, they still have the greatness within them. But, now they are called hopeless because they have lost all hope of finding their greatness.

As long as we are pulling on our greatness, we have a chance of pulling it out of us. Release the greatness that's within you. It's still there you know!

If You Believe It You Can Achieve It

•   •   •   •   •

The American Philosopher Ralph Waldo Emerson once said: "What lies behind us and what lies before us, are tiny matters compared to what lies within us." How very true this is for all of us.

No matter what we accomplished in the past, we have the ability to do more in the future. Regardless of what we plan to accomplish in the future, we have the talent within us to reach even greater heights.

The secret to releasing our inner talents lies in our belief. When you believe in you–you can achieve absolutely everything you believe you can achieve. No matter how big, no matter how small, when you believe in you–you can reach it all.

When we convince ourselves that we are going to excel, all of the greatness within us will work to bring this about. As Emerson said: "It's 'what lies within us, that really counts." So, make sure you rely on your inner strength to reach your goals in life.

When You Put It All Together You Can't Lose

• • • • •

There are thousands of real winners all over the country. Recently, I had the opportunity to watch one up close and in action.

I was at the U.S. Open Tennis Tournament at Flushing Meadow, in New York. An unseeded player named Andre Agassi unexpectedly won the tournament. He had not won a grand slam event in over two years and had little chance of winning this event. With other big names in this tournament like, Pete Sampras, Jim Courier and Michael Chang, he was not expected to do well at all.

However, Andre came to the tournament to win. He beat five seeded players before the final match. The championship match was two hours long. He made only fourteen errors. His opponent made forty eight. He kept the pressure on and won the match in straight sets (6–1, 7–6, 7–5). After the match he said: "You have to put it all together to win." Sometimes we have to use our mind, our body, and our soul to get where we want to go. When you put it all together you can't lose. Use all of your abilities to reach your full potential in life.

Handle It

· · · · ·

If you are anything like the average American, you face stressful situations daily. Stress can come from being in a traffic jam or from a project given to you at school or work or from the pressure of meeting your daily responsibilities. Even getting ready for the day can be stressful. As a matter of fact, anything can be stressful to anyone depending solely upon their level of tolerance for a given situation.

The secret is handling your stress. The way we handle stress often determines our degree of stress. There are numerous ways we can manage stress. Here are just a few: (1) Get regular exercise. (2) Laugh as much as you can. It's healthy! (3) Find an enjoyable hobby: like racquetball, tennis, knitting or reading. (4) Postpone thinking about problems. (5) Do something fun! (6) Be patient with yourself. (7) Contact an old friend, just to talk. (8) Read a novel. (9) Buy yourself a gift, for no reason at all. (10) Cry, if you have to. (11) Learn something new whenever you can. (12) Let go of any guilt you may have.

Anyone of these suggestions can help reduce stress. There are many ways to manage stress. Develop a routine that works for you.

Thoughts Per Day

• • • • •

Do you know it has been scientifically proven that we have more than 50,000 thoughts per day. Through electronic testing of brain waves, scientist have found that we average 200 negative thoughts per day. Unfortunately, one negative thought can ruin your day.

This time of year, just like any time of year, can be a time for fun and excitement. We can combat any negative thoughts with positive ones. Just say you're not going to submit to the negatives. Then think about the things that bring you joy. Do something fun or do something daring. Be determined to make yourself happy.

We have the power to control our thoughts. Over 49,000 of the 50,000 thoughts we have daily are positive. Use them to wipe–out the negative thoughts. "Enough is enough," when it comes to negative thoughts we've got to get tough.

They Have The Experience

•   •   •   •   •

Many of us realize that our senior citizen population is one of the greatest assets available to us. Seniors have a warehouse of knowledge and they are often very willing to share it with us.

My grandfather recently celebrated his ninety second birthday. Frequently, we sit and just talk about various subjects. I always leave with an abundance of knowledge. Nothing can replace experience, and "Oh Boy" is he full of experiences. We have discussed little known facts about many events that occurred early in the century, such as the great depression. He has given me increased knowledge of the first and second world wars. I have learned about events that cannot be found in history books. Like most people, he enjoys sharing his experiences and I have always enjoyed learning more about life.

If you can, talk to our senior citizens. Learn what they know. Seek their advice. Your companionship will help them, and their worldly knowledge can definitely help you.

Be At Your Peak When Things Look The Worst

• • • • •

During my high school years, I was on my school's wrestling team. We had a pretty good team and winning was our #1 priority. My good friend Linwood Murray was also on the team. He was always at his best when things looked the worst.

Linwood was an average wrestler until he was on his back. When things looked bleak greatness would shoot out of him. Anytime his opponent was about to pin him, he became a different person altogether. He would become a person that would not take defeat. He became impossible to beat and often reversed himself from a losing position to a winning position and pinned his opponent.

This trait became his trademark. He was so reliable the team frequently hoped the other wrestler would put him on his back. Quite honestly, we often rooted for his opponent until he put Linwood on his back. I don't remember Linwood ever getting pinned–He just wouldn't let it happen.

Sometimes it takes the worst situation to bring out the best in us. Life cannot pin you down if you're determined to stay on top.

Compliments

• • • • •

Don't you feel great when someone compliments you! If someone says to you I like your dress, I like your suit or I like your shoes; doesn't that make you feel good inside. Well, the same is true when you compliment someone else.

If you want to get the best out of someone, give them a "sincere" compliment. We all need positive input from others. If you want to help someone have a better day, compliment their work, compliment their attitude or compliment their personality.

We feel better and become more productive when we hear positive comments about ourselves. Compliments are so powerful, the sender will even feel better. Try giving some positive comments to your friends, co-workers or even strangers. You'll brighten someone's day and make your own day a little happier. You might even get a compliment or two in return. Do it today!

Read, Read, Read, & Read

• • • • •

Did you know that our growth and development depends on what we learn over the years? The more we learn, the greater are our chances for achievement and success. More importantly, there is no better way of learning than reading.

Yes, it's the old fashion way and it still works great. The average university student is expected to read over twenty–five books a year. Reading is the primary means for their growth and development. It has proven to be the best conduit for receiving new information.

The average American adult reads less than one book a year. Unfortunately, many of us are missing out on a great opportunity. Try reading just one book per month. It will increase your knowledge tremendously. In just one year you'll read more than the average person reads in ten years. When you read at this rate your personal growth will definitely increase. Read as much as you can, whenever you can, and watch yourself grow and develop. (In the back of this book I have listed a number of self–empowerment books I frequently recommend to my workshop participants.)

Life's Full Of Adventure And Excitement

• • • • •

As most of us know, life can appear very routine at times. Our daily schedule remains the same. The path we follow to work is unchanging. The duties required of us become repetitive. However, life can be full of excitement and exhilaration if we allow it to be.

Maya Angelou, a great poet, once said: "Because of the daily routines we follow, we often forget that life is an ongoing adventure." I agree with her 100 percent. You can find adventure at every turn when you create it.

We can drive to work by using a different route, or look for new and exciting ways to do our work. Adventure and excitement differs from person to person, so it's okay to break the routine to do the things that are adventurous to you. If you look you can find adventure in the routine things that life requires of you.

The more exciting things we do, the more rewarding life becomes. Be determined to make your day, your week and your year, full of adventure and excitement.

Plan For The Best

• • • • •

This year will be your best year ever if you plan it that way. Right now is a great time to reflect on your previous accomplishments. If you're satisfied with your level of achievement, make plans to maintain that level. If you're not satisfied, plan to achieve more as the year progresses.

Take the time to design a definite plan of action. It's essential for your personal and professional growth. Construct a detailed plan and commit it to paper. Start by writing down five or ten major goals you would like to accomplish. List them in order of importance to you. Then, below each goal, write out your plan of action to attain it.

Finally, concentrate on the details of your plans. Be as specific as you can. Leave space to add more details for future ideals. To help develop your plan, talk to people who have already accomplished what you would like to achieve and remember to put time limits on each of your actions. As you develop your plan, read and research frequently. Don't forget to review your progress at least 52 times a year!

Persistence Is One Of The Keys To Success

· · · · ·

In life there is nothing like persistence. When we are determined to reach our goals we'll reach them every time. Absolutely nothing can replace persistence. If we keep coming back, the door of opportunity is bound to open.

Sometimes everything will run smoothly the first time we attempt it, but frequently things will not always transpire perfectly. Often we must make adjustments and try again and again. The one who is persistent usually wins. We fail only when we give–up and not one moment before. As long as we are trying to attain our goals, we are making progress towards them.

If you really want to reach a goal, keep it in front of you and work sedulously at achieving it. If you don't reach it exactly as planned, keep pushing yourself towards it. Your persistence will eventually pay off. There are thousands of success stories about people who wouldn't give–up. You will be one of those thousands of people telling your success story when you persevere.

Play The Water Holes Like A Winner

• • • • •

When you come to the water holes in life you have to play them like a winner. I've watched many golfers tee off right in the water, perfectly. They unknowingly planned it that way. Anytime there is a pond between them and their destination, they talk themselves right into it.

I've heard many golfers say, "I'll never get the ball over the water", or "I always hit into the water", or even "I hate the water holes". They set themselves up to fail and nine times out of ten they fail. As a matter of fact, they were defeated before they picked up the golf club. I have watched guys take out their worst ball at the water hole. They don't want to lose their best ball. They are also planning to fail.

When we plan to fail we increase our chances of failing. When we plan to win we increase our chances of winning. Winners plan for success not failure. They concentrate on what it takes to win. Obstacles just make the challenge more interesting. Life is full of water holes. We can talk ourselves into them or we can fly right over them. Our thoughts often dictate where we will go. So, think about the positive things you want to see happen in your life and concentrate on bringing them about.

Kindness Is Like A Boomerang

• • • • •

Did you know that kindness is somewhat magical and it can fill us with all sorts of good feelings. Moreover, kindness is free and takes very little effort to give away.

Everyone appreciates kindness. Of course some of us show our appreciation and some of us don't. But, all of us like being treated kindly. When we treat someone nicely, for no special reason at all, we can touch their hearts. We can also bring out the best in them. Very few people will reject your kindness.

Furthermore, kindness is like a boomerang. When you throw it out it will come flying right back to you. If you want to develop a better relationship with someone, treat them well and say complimentary things about them. Be kind to them. If you are sincere, I guarantee you they will return what you have given to them. Kindness alone can take you a long way in life. Share as much of it as you possibly can. Others will be glad that you did.

Do The Unexpected

•　　•　　•　　•　　•

I'd like to share with you a true story about a friend of mine who works in the sales field. Early in his career he wanted to win-over lots of large clients. He would do just about anything to get their business.

One day he visited a potentially big customer to make a sale. Securing this sale was very important to him so he took his manager along for additional support. Nearing the end of his presentation, to this prospective client, he knew things were not going well. He had not convinced the client to accept his offer. He gave a fine presentation and there was very little his manager could add to make it any better.

Towards the end of his presentation the client interrupted his closing remarks and said "How do I know that you will satisfy our needs." My friend got up out of his seat, walked to the corner of the room and actually stood on his head. Everyone in the room looked at him in amazement. Then he returned to his seat and said: "We will stand on our heads to satisfy you." The client gave him that contract and many more. Sometimes we have to do the unexpected to get what we expect in life.

Keep Your Dreams Close To You

• • • • •

Are you living your dreams? Are you doing the things that make you happy? If your answer is yes, congratulations, you have found what most people are looking for. You have found the key to living a successful life.

Everyone can live their dreams. That's been proven time and time again. Many folks, with all sorts of adversities, live full and complete lives. They don't let anything stop them from living life completely. They turn adversity into prosperity. They break all chains that bind them. They are determined to change their dreams into reality.

Whatever your dreams may be, live them. Be determined to make them come true. Think of them frequently. Work to make them a reality. Let nothing separate you and your dreams. If you keep your dreams close to you, they will become a part of you.

If your dreams are worth dreaming, never ever throw them away. Your dreams often become your reality. So, dream big and dream often!

Stay Loose

• • • • •

We all know that it's impossible to predict the outcome of every ordeal we encounter. Sometimes things turn-out exactly as we wish. Other times we are not pleased at all with the outcomes we encounter. One key to handling every event we are confronted with is being flexible.

Flexibility allows us to handle the unpredictable situations that we will face from time to time. When events don't unfold as planned a flexible nature will allow us to adjust as needed. After we adjust we can keep moving forward. If there is no give and take, we often become stuck whenever a problem comes along. Our forward progress can be severely hampered.

Most of us prefer to associate with people who can easily adapt to changing situations. No matter how perfect our plans are we have to be ready to adjust them, if necessary. One major key to success is our ability to handle and adapt to a changing environment. Our level of flexibility will influence the level of our success. Since our plans don't always turn out as intended, flexibility is a must. Stay loose!

Show Your Courage

• • • • •

Did you know that it takes courage to live life completely. We never know what each day will bring. Courage gives us the strength to handle everything that befalls us. For some of us courage comes naturally. For others, we have to build it day by day. Courage absolutely makes a difference in our entire life. When we have it, our days become an adventure. With courage we're not easily intimidated, and we become excited about new and different opportunities. Doors open all around us and we are not afraid to walk through them.

Everyone has courage. Some of us have to spend time developing it, but, it's there in all of us. Just as we exercise our muscles to make them stronger, we often have to exercise our courage to develop it. So, do courageous things daily. Do things you normally wouldn't do. Ask for a pay raise, speak up in class, or join that weight loss program.

Being courageous means different things to different people. Whenever you do something you normally wouldn't do, you're showing your courage.

Just One-percent

• • • • •

Did you know that most people don't reach their full potential in life. It is a proven fact that ninety–nine percent of us fail to reach our full potential. That means that only one percent of us achieve what we are able to achieve in life. Incredible huh!

It would be unrealistic to expect everyone to reach their full potential. But one percent seems a bit low. That's just one out of every one hundred people. We have to wonder why that one person reaches their full potential and the rest do not.

Fortunately, countless studies have been conducted to determine why this phenomenon exist. The conclusion of most studies point to one thing. That one thing is attitude. Not aptitude! Not environment! Not training! Attitude is the answer. One Harvard University study revealed that 85% of the reasons for success were because of attitude. It allows us to grow to our ability. It's like the path beneath our feet. It's our light that shines in the darkness. The more positive our attitude the greater are our chances of reaching our full potential. The one percent of people that are high achievers keep their attitude in peak shape. To reach your full potential keep your attitude pointed in the right direction.

Let It Go

•   •   •   •   •

Sometimes in life we have to let go of one thing to gain another. Too often we try to move forward without letting go of the past. We end up trying to run a forty yard dash with an extra one hundred pounds of baggage on our backs.

Of course we can run the race, but, there is little chance of winning. Removing the extra weight is the smart thing to do. Once you have completed a project or a phase in your life, let it go. When you make a decision don't look back. What's done is done. When we dwell on the past, it slows our future growth. Make a decision and move beyond it. Right or wrong, the decision has been made. If you have to change it, change it, and then move on.

There's an old saying: "You can't steal second base with one foot on first base." When we want to move ahead we have to let go of those things that are keeping us back. Run your races in life without the extra weight on your back. You'll increase your chance of winning.

Opportunities Frequently Visit Us

• • • • •

Do you know that great things are coming your way? All of us experience opportunities throughout our lifetime. Some of them are large and some are small, but they always come our way. As a matter of fact, at this very moment an opportunity is coming your way.

We must constantly prepare ourselves for the opportunities that will appear. When we're not prepared the occasion can slip away. Conversely, when we are prepared great things can happen. A basketball coach will call upon his best players to take the critical shots. The best players have prepared for the opportunities and opportunities always come their way.

It's better to prepare for a challenge before the challenge arrives. It's too late to prepare when the opportunity is at your doorstep. In life, perfect opportunities for our growth, development, and success frequently visit us. Sometimes they're as easy to see as fireworks in the sky. Other times, they're not so clearly displayed. Decide what you want to accomplish in life. Prepare to do it. Then look out for the opportunity. It will be coming your way.

Give Up The Small Stuff

•　　•　　•　　•　　•

Temporary sacrifice can bring about great rewards. If there are important things that we want to acquire in life, sometimes temporary sacrifice, of less important things, is the best way to bring our desires to us.

Sacrificing can be difficult. It usually means that we have to give up something we enjoy. However, we usually sacrifice one thing to gain something more fulfilling. For example, if we would like to save some of our money to buy something special like; a new wardrobe, a car or a house, we might have to dine–out less often or sacrifice that exotic vacation this year in order to attain it.

In life, we often give up one thing to gain another. Sacrificing is a temporary adjustment which can lead you to perpetual long term gain. It often means releasing the "small stuff" to acquire the "big stuff." Practice small sacrifices and let them lead you to the large accomplishments. Develop the habit of giving up less important things so that you can focus on the more important and fulfilling things life has to offer.

The Optimistic Route

• • • • •

Pure optimism can take us everywhere we want to go in life. Whenever we're optimistic, the doors of opportunity fly open everywhere we choose to go. It's really quite funny, when we plan for positive things to occur, they regularly occur. When we expect the worst, sadly, that can also appear.

Be Optimistic! Expect the best in your life. It's an easy decision and it really affects the outcome of your life. We have absolutely nothing to lose by being optimistic. One of the greatest boxers of all times, Muhammad Ali, once said: "To be a great champion you must believe you are the best."

Ali's optimism helped to develop him into a premier champion. Optimism will surely help you become great at whatever you choose to do. Start every project with the end result in your mind. Believe that the result you seek will be perfect. Then, work towards perfection. When we take the optimistic route the doors of opportunity will fly open again and again. Choose the optimistic route as you travel down the roadway of life.

Only One Way To Go

• • • • •

Have you ever felt that you have fallen to your lowest point; that things were so bad that they couldn't get any worst? Well, when you're at the bottom of the heap or at the end of your rope, there's only one way to go and that one way is up.

When we are at the lowest point or near the bottom there's plenty of room above us. Perhaps you have heard it before, there's a silver lining in every cloudy situation. It's okay to take a few seconds to feel sorry about the situation, but, don't spend much more than a few seconds feeling sorry. There's work to be done.

Each leap we take forward is a leap towards success. All of our thoughts should be conspiring to move forward. The more we concentrate on this effort the greater our forward leap will become. If we are moving ahead, it is absolutely impossible to go backwards.

No matter what our troubles, there is a viable solution awaiting. Focusing on moving forward will bring that solution to us. When we're at the bottom or at the end of the rope, there's only one way to go and that way is up. The thing to do is move in that direction.

Personal Change

• • • • •

Whenever we personally change our thinking or change our habits, for the better, we implement a positive personal change in our life. Positive changes obviously are most beneficial in our quest to achieve more out of life. If you would like to learn additional powerful lessons about personal change I recommend reading The Seven Habits of Highly Effective People by Stephen Covey (in addition to The Struggle Stops Here, by yours truly, of course).

In his best selling book, Covey discusses everything from attitude to imagination. He outlines the importance of having a mission in life and shows you how to follow it. He takes a good look at interpersonal development and discusses the importance of a win/win philosophy. He shows us how to begin our quest for a better life and how to continue it.

Covey reviewed over 200 years of success literature before completing The Seven Habits of Highly Effective People. It's truly an exciting book on personal development. All whom take the time to read it will benefit greatly.

The Proper Background

• • • • •

It's not uncommon for someone from a modest or even hope-less background to excel in life. In many cases, the more disad-vantaged the background of a person the greater the chances of mega success. Here's just one example.

Lee Trevino is one the best and most respected golfers in the history of the game. He has won just about every major award the sport has to offer. Most would think that a poor young eighth grade drop-out would have no chance of making it; particularly not in the "game of preference" for many world leaders. But, the fact that many people thought he didn't have a chance became his motivation to succeed.

In the early morning when others were asleep Trevino was on the practice tee hitting hundreds of golf balls. In the evening when other golfers celebrated the day's end with a drink at the club, he was again on the practice tee hitting balls. His back-ground gave him very little to lose. So, he knew very early in life he had everything to gain. Like many high achievers Trevino real-ized that a disadvantaged background can be your greatest asset in life if you use the experience in a positive way.

You've Got The Power

• • • • •

It's a fact that all of us have the power to accomplish anything we choose to accomplish. There is an organ approximately five inches above your neck, two inches behind your eyes and right smack between your ears. It weighs approximately three pounds, is the most powerful thing on earth, and it never stops working exclusively for you.

Yes, I'm talking about your brain. It is the most complicated thing on earth and would cost billions of dollars to duplicate. Each of us has been given one free of charge. When used correctly it becomes an extremely powerful tool for us. It's been used to fly us to the moon, build enormous skyscrapers and help us communicate from one side of the earth to the other in a matter of seconds.

Many scientist agree that the mind has infinite wisdom and power. There is just no limit to what it can do. Challenge your mind to solve any problem and in time, it will. As long as we have a brain we have an abundance of power. There is no such thing as a powerless human being, only those who choose not to use that remarkable organ between their ears.

Ride It Out

• • • • •

Life is full of surprises some are good and some are bad. When the good times come we should take the time to enjoy it. When the tough times arrive we sometimes just have to ride out the storm.

One summer a few years ago, some associates and myself were sailing on the Chesapeake Bay enjoying a lovely afternoon. The sun was shining and there wasn't a cloud in the sky. It seemed to be a perfect day and we were having a great time on our small vessel. All of a sudden seemingly from nowhere bad weather rapidly moved upon us. The sky became dark. It started to drizzle. We immediately began to secure the boat. It became obvious that we were going to be pounded by a severe thunderstorm.

It was too late to sail for cover. We had to "ride it out". Shortly after reefing the sails and putting on our foul weather gear, the winds picked- up and the thunder and lighting appeared with a down-pour of rain. The calm waters became angry waves pounding our boat.

Everyone remained focused and worked diligently to keep the boat on course. In less than thirty minutes the storm had passed. In less than an hour the sun peaked out again. We had survived a major storm. Because we stuck to our guns, the storm didn't defeat us. It's true – tough times never last when you're tough enough to ride it out.

Mind, Body & Soul

• • • • •

Humans are made of three major components, the mind, the body and the soul. Each one of these attributes must be developed in order for us to become whole and complete. Our intellect is developed through the mind. Our physical well being is developed through the body. Our spiritual well being is developed through our soul.

We will not be completely developed unless all three of these areas are developed. The mind is home to our intellect which helps us to decipher all with which we come into contact. The body is the coordinator of our mobility on earth. Without its strength our movement would be limited. The soul is where we house our true self. Here we'll find what influences our mind and body most.

A well developed mind, body and soul is the key to life long and eternal happiness. Working on developing each one should be a part of our daily routine. Incorporate activities in your life that will help you grow in each of these areas.

You Can't Please Everyone

•　•　•　•　•

In life you'll meet many different types of people. Some good some bad. Some happy, some sad. Some short and some tall. If you're around long enough you'll meet them all.

Generally, different people have differing views. For example: the tall like high door openings (for obvious reasons), the short like lower windows on their doors. The skinny like light weight doors that are easy to push. The large folks like wide openings to walk through. No matter what type of door you design, you'll make someone unhappy when you build one. And, if you try to please everyone you'll surely fail.

Therefore, we sometimes have to build things in life that are simply pleasing to us alone. Whenever we attempt to satisfy everyone's needs we are often the ones that lose. If pleasing ourselves also means pleasing thousands of others, that's great. If pleasing ourselves means pleasing only a few, well, that's OK too. When setting your goals or making your plans, help as many folks as you can, but, remember it's impossible to please everyone.

Learn It Now

• • • • •

My first job after graduating high school was as a construction laborer for my grandfather's construction company. Since I was young and had a "strong back" I got the honors of pushing a wheel–barrel, loaded with cement, most of the day.

In high school, I could think of nothing else but getting out of school to earn money for the things that I thought were important. (i.e. clothes, hamburgers, a pool cue and gas for my car). After three months of hard labor, I realized that school wasn't so bad at all; and learning to operate a business was much better than pushing wheel barrels of cement all day.

So, I decided to enroll in college to study the administration of business. Unfortunately, I didn't prepare for college level work. So, I found myself struggling to make up for the time I spent "funning" in high school. If I had listened to my elders when they said "study hard" or "do your homework," college would have been much easier. Instead, I found myself spending an hour doing the work my classmates accomplished in forty–five minutes. I often played "catch–up" with much of my coursework. If you're in school, concentrate on doing well. Save the fun for the weekend. Think about the cars, clothes and being cool later. You'll never really have the time to make up what you miss. Reserve your future for learning new things, not things you missed the first time around.

Peace, Harmony & Happiness Through God

•   •   •   •   •

How can one write a book on motivation or inspiration without acknowledging God and his greatness? Personally, I don't know how that can be done. All of my inspiration comes from God. I truly believe he will use each of us to inspire others. God loves you! He loves all of his children and wants peace, harmony and happiness to prevail in our lives.

One of the most rewarding things a person can do is get to know God. When we understand his wants and desires we will have a better chance of achieving our wants and desires. If our aspirations are in conflict with God's wishes, we are sure to fail. However, when we move in conjunction with God and his teachings we have His infinite power and wisdom transporting us ahead.

All of your plans for success are futile if God, the greatest planner, motivator and inspirer, is not leading the way. HE IS THE TRUTH, THE LIGHT, the path beneath our feet and our shining star in the sky. Trust in his wisdom.

Winning On The Inside First

• • • • •

For years they were considered one of the worst teams in the league. They had not been in contention for a championship spot in recent history. As a matter of fact, other teams discarded their presence when they were on the playing field. At the beginning of the 1995 football season many critics voted the San Diego Chargers most likely to end the season in last place, but the Chargers had another scenario in mind. Throughout the season, they shocked football fans all over the country. After the regular playing season, everyone agreed that the Chargers had an exceptional year. However, very few thought they would have any chance of winning against the dream busting Pittsburgh Steelers in Three River Stadium. The Chargers ignored their critics. They came to the Steelers' homefield to snatch the dream from the dream snatchers and they did just that as they won the AFC championship.

After the game, player after player on the Chargers' team said "We knew we were going to win." When you erase all doubts of failing there's little chance left of failing. Most of the time, we have to win inside our hearts before we can win on the playing field.

You Depending On You

• • • • •

Our entire country is moving towards self-empowerment. The federal government is cracking down on its funding of special programs to help needy citizens. State and local governments don't have the resources to pick up the slack. So, the onus is being placed upon individuals to better provide for themselves.

I have been fortunate enough to make over one hundred television appearances promoting self–efficacy and self–development. There is no better time to fire up our attitudes. We need to believe, now more than ever, in ourselves and in our God-given abilities. We can no longer depend on the government or any other support system to always be there. Reductions in spending seems to become vastly deeper with each succeeding year. They will touch all of us, someday.

If we are firm in our belief in ourselves and work persistently to better ourselves and to improve our marketability, harsh economical conditions will have less of an impact on us. Self–efficacy has always been the key to success. In good times and in bad times; what you have inside of you will absolutely see you through.

The Team

• • • • •

One person can achieve plenty at work, at home or at his advocation. Naturally, two people working together can achieve more than one working alone. Moreover, a team of three or more people working together, for the same goals, can accomplish a tremendous amount. Why not assemble a team to help you reach your aspirations in life. You'll enhance your overall plans for success.

Start with your family and get all of them on board, if you can. Let them know what you plan to accomplish. Help them to understand how important it is to you. As you solicit their support, clearly explain how they can be beneficial to the team. Explain the team concept and have positive rewards for their participation (a hug or a kiss may be all that they require). Let them know that your plans will benefit everyone and be sure to share your success.

Seek additional team members from your friendships. Make it rewarding to be a member of your team. Sell them on your ideas. Then, talk to your associates. Choose those people who can help you reach your goals. Bring key players to your team. You're the coach and the star player. Now lead your team to victory.

Stand Out From The Crowd

• • • • •

Sometimes in life we have to stand out from the crowd. There is safety in numbers, but there is also anonymity. Being anonymous will not make us a star or get us noticed by those who may employ our services. Whenever the promotional opportunities come along, standing out in the crowd will get us noticed. Doing the same thing the crowd chooses to do will reap us the same rewards as the others. But, stepping out and taking those chances can bring greater rewards our way.

If we stay within the parameters of the organizational climate, but, do things a little differently (or better) than others, we'll get positive recognition. Exciting new assignments will appear and drift your way. Most organizations are by nature risk taking entities. Their start was a risk. The daily operations are a risk. Every change it makes is a risk. When we do things a little differently, we are also taking a risk. Our success will fit perfectly into the business climate.

Stand outside of the crowd whenever you can. Let there be no anonymity for you. Let your unique way of producing be the standard others try to reach. Be the leader of the pack not the one who follows the pack.

A Perfect Balancing Act

• • • • •

Nature has a way of keeping itself in balance throughout the universe. Balance is nature's key to creating harmony and renewing vitality among all things that inhabit earth; both plants and animals alike. Without a balance there would be discord everywhere. Can you image snow falling in July or zero degree temperature in the middle of August? Certainly, both are fairly hard to comprehend.

Nature has a reason for balancing the blossoming of the trees, the rate of rainfall, the way in which the wind blows and a host of other natural occurrences. Too much of any one thing, or the untimely appearance of another, can off–set the balance of nature. Occasionally rivers overflow or the wind blows too hard. This is nature again going through a process of checks and balances.

Human existence is a part of nature's balancing act. We require sleep, we must work to survive, we enjoy leisure time. If we spend too much time doing any one of the above, we create an imbalance that can be detrimental. But, if we follow the path nature planned for us we will succeed at living a well balanced life.

Seeds Of Greatness

• • • • •

Motivational seminars, workshops and talks are an excellent way to help us sharpen our self development skills. I attend such learning opportunities frequently. All of us are a sum total of what goes into our minds and bodies. Whatever we put in we can harvest in return. If we choose to put only junk or other wasteful things inside of us, we should be cautious of what we expect to produce. However, if we plant the seeds of greatness only greatness will sprout out of us. An apple seed will only produce an apple, an orange seed will only produce an orange. The seeds of greatness will only produce greatness.

When we learn those things that are necessary or fundamental to our successful growth, we create a fertile environment in which our minds can grow and develop. We never stop learning. It's well known that many successful persons started great ventures in the latter portion of their lives. Experienced teachers in the area of self development can help hone our skills and bring out the best in us. External intervention is often required as we seek success in life. Perhaps you have heard these mindful sayings before: "No man is an island" or "there is no need to reinvent the wheel."

Restore The Hope

• • • • •

Throughout the nation hundreds of our children are being killed every year. Our inner cities have literally become "war zones." The crackling of gun fire is common place as the glimmering sunlight fades to a smoldering darkness on many of our streets. Sadly, kids dropping to their knees, grasping a deadly wound, seems to be a more likely fate than grabbing a diploma on the graduation stage of a major university.

Hopelessness has become the evil creature that entangles too many of our youth today. It sucks their dreams down into the sewers. Because they feel there is no hope in trying to "make it" as a sports hero or a wall street tycoon, their hope lies in drugs, guns, and other serious criminal activity. Unfortunately, this becomes the hope of the hopeless.

All is not lost. The parents, teachers, counselors and other caring individuals can make a significant difference. We cannot afford to give up our fight against their hopelessness. When we restore the hope of one child we help to restore the hope of a generation of children. Our success in life greatly depends on our surrounding the environment in which we live. When we help a struggling child to become an asset to his environment, we help to develop our entire environment.

The #1 Plan

• • • • •

Have you created your Master Plan? The master plan is the one your life is based upon. We all have plans. Some of us plan to buy a new car. Some of us plan to buy a house. Some of us just plan to buy (I'm referring to the shop until you drop crowd). Whatever the case may be, less than five–percent of us have a formal plan for success: A plan by which we can live our entire life.

Our formal plan for life is our "Master Plan." We cannot attain long term success without it. Every successful person I have ever met has a master plan and follows it diligently. With a master plan in mind we recognize the correct paths to follow as we travel through life. We have a basis for all of the important decisions that come our way.

A person's master plan will include personal, professional as well as financial goals. It will give him adequate time to reach those goals. It will allow for flexibility in case changes must be incorporated as we grow and develop. And, most importantly, it will include step by step measures to reach each goal that is set.

Born Leader

• • • • •

We are the King, President, Leader and Chief Executive. We alone are the sole executor of our own free will. We alone ultimately choose to perform or not perform. Whenever a decision comes our way we independently decide what our reaction will be. Certainly others can persuade us. They can convince us to act in a certain manner. But, the actual decision to respond or not to respond is ours. Even children choose to react to their parent's command or requests. It is the child's decision to act in accordance with his parents wishes. The parent is not making the decision the child is. The adult merely uses persuasion.

Since we are in charge of our actions, we are definitely the King, President, Leader, and Chief Executive of our lives. We are all born with this authority. We were born decision makers. If we don't remain great it is because we choose (consciously or subconsciously) not to do so. If we have lost our greatness and would like to see it returned, we should put constant effort into restoring it everyday. We can start with building our belief in our own ability. Believing that we were born great and that, that greatness is still within us. Then, we can start to revitalize the great attributes within us; such as our faith, talents, love, decisiveness, honor, sincerity, etc...

There Are No Average People

• • • • •

Do you know that you are invincible. You can defeat everything that stands between you and your success. All of us have the talent and the inert skills to overcome our difficulties. If we didn't have this ability we could not survive on the planet earth. Man has overcome every obstacle placed in his path. Even dinosaurs, one of earth's greatest monstrosities to mankind, were not able to wipe man from the earth. They instead fell to extinction as man rose to greatness. We have a propensity for excelling. Each century man becomes more in tune to his infinite ability to succeed.

Man has been given more than just survival skills. We have been given the skills to surpass any difficulty obstructing our path. The more we hear about great deeds being performed by so called "average people", we have to come to realize that there are no average people; only great people who may think they're average. Our inner greatness makes us invincible to all things that attempt to suppress us. As long as we remember that we carry our greatness with us everywhere we travel in life, we can rely on it to help us whenever we desire. Learn to tap into the greatness within you.

There's Is No "Powerlessness" In America

• • • • •

America is considered one of the greatest countries on earth, if not the greatest. The "poorest" in our society would be considered wealthy in many impoverished nations. In America the poor and seemingly defeated have a chance to excel. As a matter of fact, there are many opportunities for anyone to excel. Many channels leading toward success are firmly intact. And where there are no channels we can develop the ingenuity to create them. In many foreign nations there are few channels and very little leverage is available for the average citizen to create advancement opportunities. Only the wealthy can acquire an education or other resources necessary to advance themselves.

As Americans we should constantly take advantage of every resource available to aid us in our growth. We should not consider ourselves poor when we have such an abundance available to us. Thinking poor, hopeless or lost will only lead us to a feeling of powerlessness. Feeling powerless drains our desire to pursue our excellence. All Americans have power.

The power here for us is in such abundance, the whole world is trying to get a piece of it. Just go to any border state and ask why they have a border patrol. It's not to keep Americans from leaving,

I assure you. Many of us have forgotten how to utilize our power or we have been brainwashed into believing we're powerless. When we commit ourselves to POWERFULNESS, as opposed to POWERLESSNESS we reopen the "doors of opportunity." The next step is to walk through those doors and claim our riches.

The Creativity Factor

• • • • •

The biggest doors to success lies within us. Outside factors will always influence our life. They can help or hurt our growth and progress. However, all that we require to succeed, without a doubt, lies just below our skin. If we put ourselves in a success mode, we learn to attract nothing but success to us.

As far as we know mankind is the most creative creature in the universe. Relying on our creativity can extend great opportunities to us. When we trust in our own ability we free our creative nature. Nothing materializes without first being an idea. Great ideas come from the free expression of our inner creativity. Some of the best and most creative ideas have come from what most would consider ordinary people. Their creative ideas helped them become great men or great women.

It is wise to liberate your creativeness and allow it to surface. Major companies have what is known as brainstorming sessions to encourage the liberation of the thought process.

They place groups of people together to focus on and discuss a particular topic or subject. The creative juices often flow freely and substantial positive consequences result. If it works for billion dollar corporations it can certainly work for you.

A Wealth Of Richness

• • • • •

We all are rich! All of us have an abundance of wealth. Some of us have a wealth of knowledge. Some of us possess a wealth of talent at a particular endeavor. Others have a wealth of good health. In our society, we too quickly equate richness and wealth with monetary or material accumulation. Personal material accumulation is only one type of wealth. It's certainly debatable as to whether or not it is the most important type of wealth.

A man with poor health lying on his death bed would probably give all of his monetary and material wealth just to possess a fraction of the good health we may retain. A man with lots of money, but a deteriorating mind would graciously trade some of his money for a small piece of your sanity. Most of us have been blessed with a sound body and mind, but too many of us take these blessings for granted and overlook these riches we acquired at birth. It is the man who fails to respect his inner riches who never finds the additional richness in life. The wise man uses the wealth of inner richness he currently possesses to help him find additional riches in the world.

Fundamentals

• • • • •

Most of us want a better and more prosperous life. We want to live in a larger or newer house or live in a more affluent neighborhood. We frequently want a more expensive car or a finer wardrobe. We always want more money in our pockets or bank accounts. We often want most of the finer things life has to offer. And, why shouldn't we desire and acquire these niceties. One of the reasons why you're reading this book is because you're seeking to improve your life.

Everyone can have a more abundant and more fulfilling life. It's available to each of us. That's no secret! Several of the keys to a better life has been given to you many times throughout this writing. In case you missed the fundamental ones, here they are again.

1. Believe in your ability to achieve anything you desire.

2. Develop a strong desire to win or to reach your goals.

3. Set your goals before you do anything else.

4. Work hard at achieving your goals.

5. Find a mentor and let them show you the way to a successful encounter.

6. Attitude, attitude, attitude and attitude.

7. Seek support from a spiritual source. (In the long run success is not worth having without supreme support.)

8. Smell the roses along the way.

9. Be careful about what you say to yourself. Your subconscious mind will act on it as if it were factual.

10. Knowledge is power – learn as much as you can about your area of interest, then apply what you have learned.

Swift And Immediate Action

•　　•　　•　　•　　•

I have lived in the mid–eastern part of the country most of my life. Every winter, that I can remember, we received at least one "major" snowfall. As the snowfall approached the area, the weathermen gave their predictions; "The harsher the prediction the greater the panic." Due to a "mad rush" on food stores, frequently the stores would run out of basic foods such as bread and milk. Lines at gas stations would suddenly appear and video stores would rent out all of their best tapes in less than a few hours. All of this because of the anticipation of a snowfall that would last, in most cases, less than eight hours. Usually in less than a day all would be back to normal except for a few inches of white stuff covering the ground. Rarely would any serious inconvenience last more than twenty– four hours.

However, the anticipation of "severe" snowfall puts people into action – it raised their consciousness about what could happen if they didn't act. The end result was swift and immediate action. For the most part there was little or no hesitation – people just acted. If we treat our goals in life in the same fashion, if we worked as if we had only a limited amount of time before the blizzard arrived, or as if nothing were more important than getting a particular task completed, we could accomplish more in life. Our tenacity will lead us to the completion of every one of our goals, bring many of our projects to immediate fruition and many additional rewards would come to our doorstep.

Pretend there's a blizzard coming your way whenever you have an important assignment to complete. Don't let anything change your focus. Do everything you must do before the deadline (blizzard) arrives.

Endurance

•　　•　　•　　•　　•

A tree will not stop growing upon being blown around in a vigorous thunderstorm. Grass scorched away by the intense heat of a hot summer day will return to its original richness and glory after the rains return. Flowers frozen into a death like state during a harsh winter season, will sprout up at the heavens just as soon as the warm spring weather arrives. The trees, the grass and the flowers never give up – they just hold on until more favorable times come. They somehow know that the devastation is just a temporary set back.

Try to think of your biggest problem just twenty-four months ago. Chances are you'll have some difficulty remembering it. What was once considered so devastating is now just a passing memory. We have gone beyond the challenges of yesterday. We survived! As we look back the problems of our past don't seem nearly as enormous as they once felt.

Troubles always arrive and depart the airports of our lives. When we endure the temporary set backs that trouble can bring and realize that greater things are ahead of us, we will continue to grow. Life is a journey full of triumphs and defeats. The defeats only last as long as we allow them to. Like the trees, grass and flowers we will also endure every hardship that comes our way.

Spiritually Grounded

· · · · ·

Some of us trust in our physical strength to bring our desires to us. Some of us trust in the keenness of our mind to beckon success to us. Others depend on friends and wealthy relatives. All of the above can be beneficial in our pursuit of greatness, but, the power of God is infinite and without it our range of success is limited. We need to become spiritually grounded as we seek to release the riches that are stored within us. The spiritual soundness that is at the very core of every human being is the conduit with which God channels his unending greatness to us. The more solid our spiritual foundation the more easily His blessings are bestowed upon us.

When we build a structure that is consistent with the objectives we seek, everything flows smoothly. When we build a dam that retards the flow only trickles of greatness can flow our way.

"Some trust in their war chariots and others trust in their houses, but, we trust in the power of the Lord our God." (Psalm 20:7)

Bearing The Load

• • • • •

Life doesn't always give us exactly what we want. Success does not always come simply because we call upon it. However, when we "bear the load," or fight off the urge to quit, our desires make their way to our reality. Often too many of us give in just a split second too soon and our hopes and dreams go sliding away never to be seen again. Life belongs to those who hold on and ride during troubled times. When we come to the full realization that the storms of trouble in our lives, are just a clearing process making the way for a miraculous sun filled day, we will understand why it is necessary to find the strength to hold on until the bad times move away.

When we bear the load we are simply enduring until brighter times come our way. Often the load seems too awesome to control. It seems to over-run us, leaving us feeling hopeless. When we give up, it is then that hardships are most apt to crush us. We must often find the strength from within to work through the tough times, day by day.

Suggested Reading

• • • • •

THE STRUGGLE STOPS HERE

. . . . Michael R. Clark

THE SEVEN HABITS OF HIGHLY EFFECTIVE PEOPLE

. . . . Stephen Covey

LIVE YOUR DREAMS

. . . . Les Brown

TOTAL SELF CONFIDENCE

. . . . Dr. Robert Anthony

THE POWER OF YOUR SUBCONSCIOUS MIND

. . . . Joseph Murphy

THE GREATEST MIRACLE IN THE WORLD

. . . . OG Mandino

SUCCESS THROUGH A POSITIVE MENTAL ATTITUDE

. . . . Napoleon Hill
W. Clement Stone

Michael R. Clark
Biographical Sketch

• • • • •

Michael R. Clark is the former Host of "MOTIVATIONAL MINUTE" a daily self–empowerment television segment aired on WBAL–TV in the Baltimore – Washington D.C. area. He is the author of "THE STRUGGLE STOPS HERE", a dynamic self–empowerment book designed to deliver "fundamental keys to success" to African Americans and other minorities. He is also the creator of "S.T.A.R. – THE HIDDEN POWER WITHIN YOU" a motivational tape series hosted by Malik Yoba, star of FOX – TV's New York Undercover.

Clark credits his sedulous reading of personal development books, early in life and attending self– empowerment seminars and workshops throughout his career for launching him from a struggling under–achiever to a highly successful over–achiever. Some of his professional accomplishments include: Becoming a nationally recognized consultant, President of a multi–million dollar corporation, marketing firm Owner, Project Manager for the construction of one of America's largest Red Cross blood pro-cessing facilities, television personality, law firm marketing spe-cialist and orator.

In addition, Michael R. Clark is listed in the international edition of the Who's Who Directory and is currently on the Board of numerous organizations. Throughout his professional career he has been an active member of over twenty–five different non–profit organizations. To help satisfy his seemingly insatiable appetite for helping others, Clark, in August of 1994 created the B.S.E.T. PROGRAM; a self–empowerment training program designed to help non–working individuals develop skills necessary to improve their lifestyles.

Clark graduated from the University of Maryland, College Park in 1979 and is currently contracted by the State of Maryland, Department of Juvenile Justice, to design and initiate the implementation of a personal development program for over 600 Baltimore City youth. Clark is an avid sailor, golfer, tennis player, and reader.

Notes

. . . . .

Notes

• • • • •

Notes

· · · · ·

Notes

Notes